EXCURSIONS

by ELVINA PEARCE

12 Original Piano Solos for Early-Level Pianists

CONTENTS

Editor: Gail Lew
Production Coordinator: Sheryl Rose
Cover Design: Thais Yanes

PREFACE

These pieces offer refreshing and exciting repertoire that goes beyond five-finger positions and motivates students to excel. Here is innovative repertoire that utilizes pedal to help create big sounds. The descriptive titles are designed to capture the imagination and nurture interpretive skills. The pieces sound harder than they are and will give students a profound sense of accomplishment.

Royal March

ELVINA PEARCE

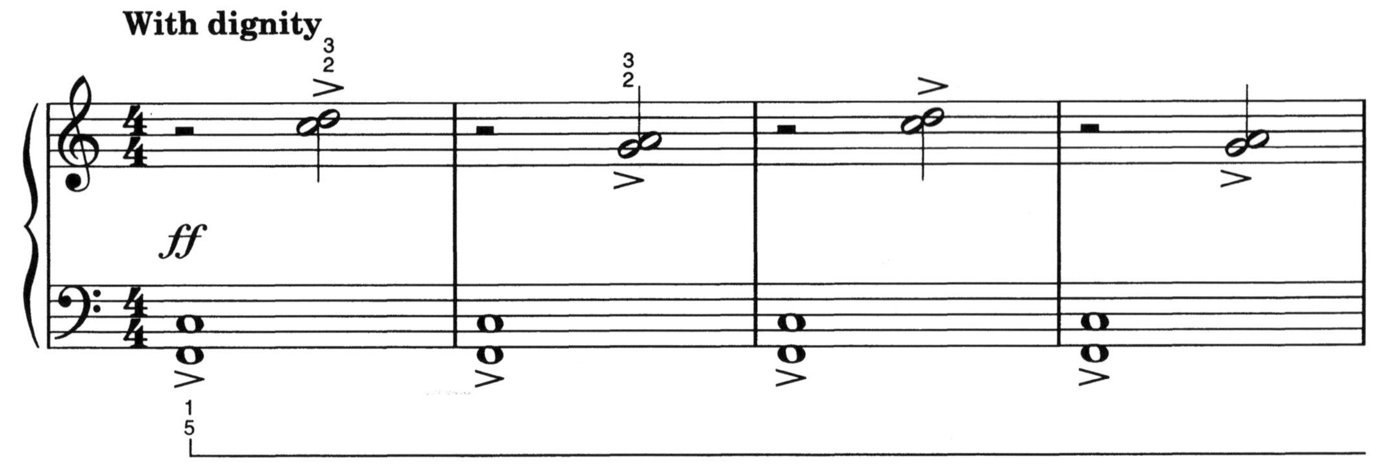

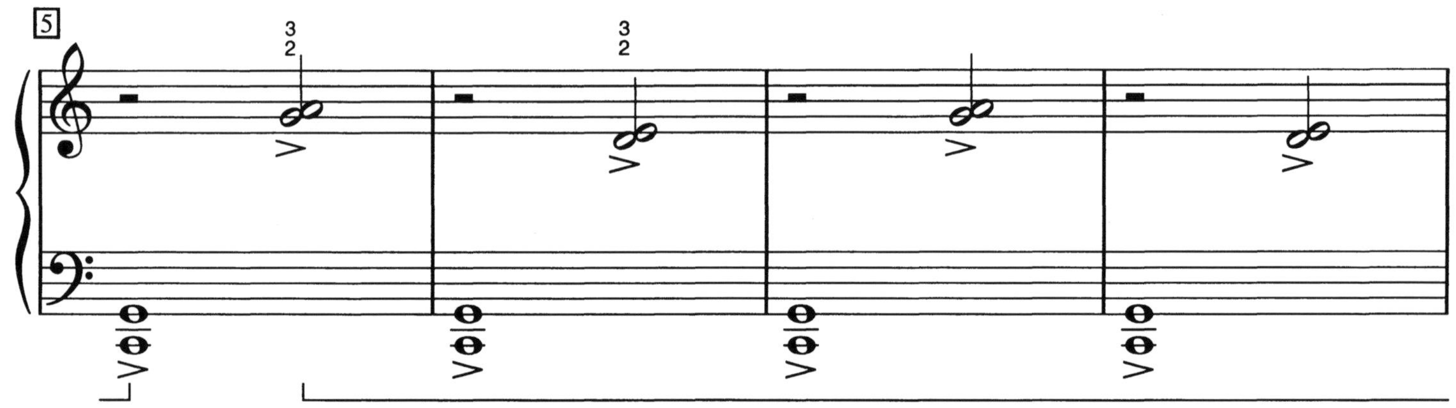

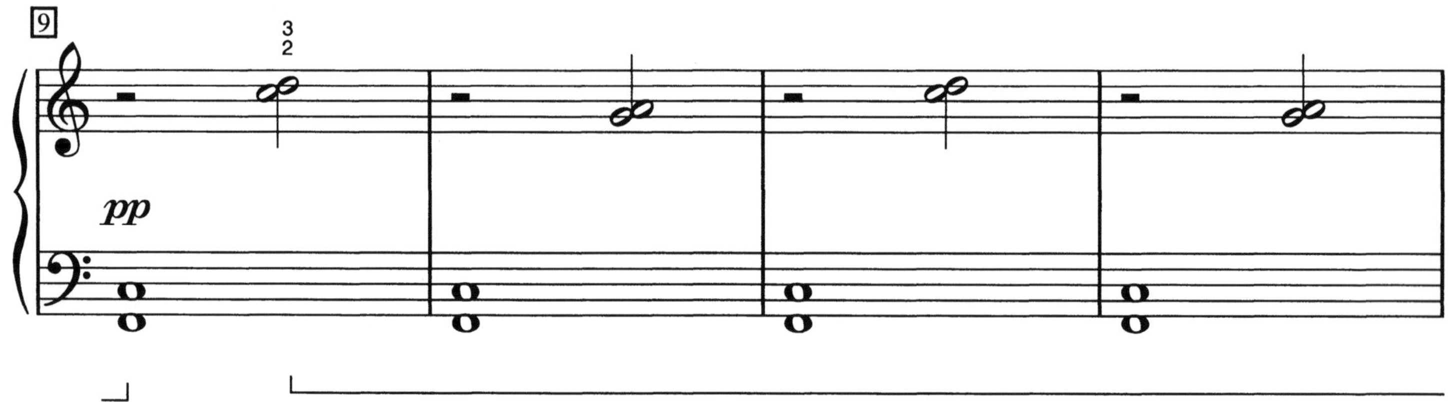

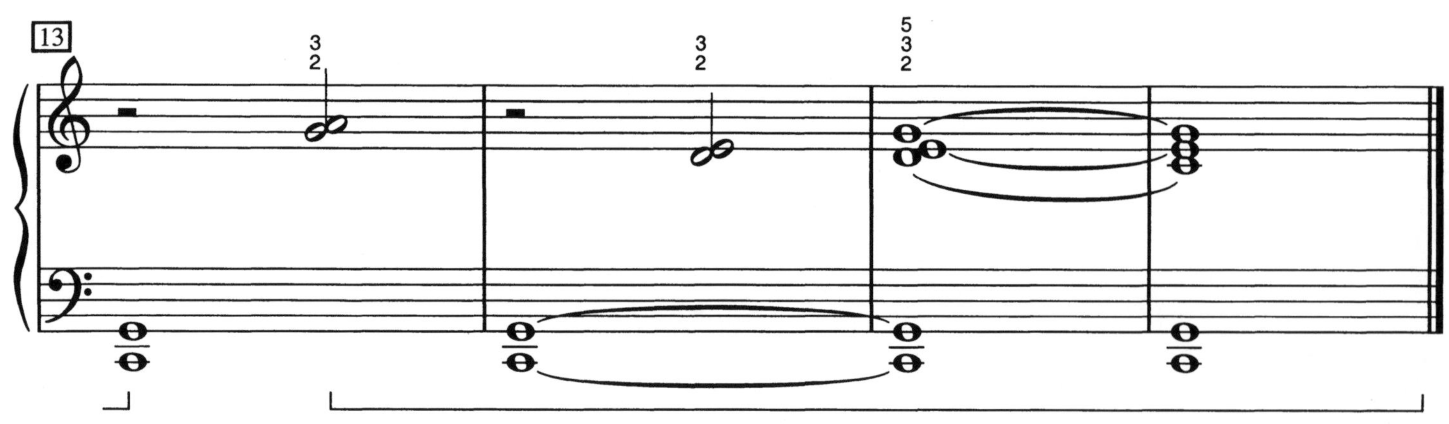

Rolling Along

ELVINA PEARCE

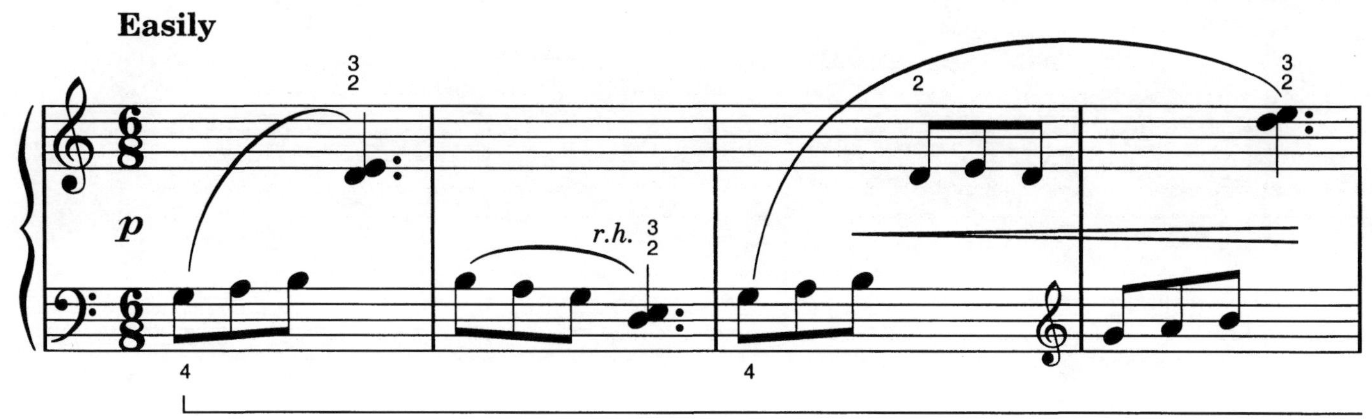

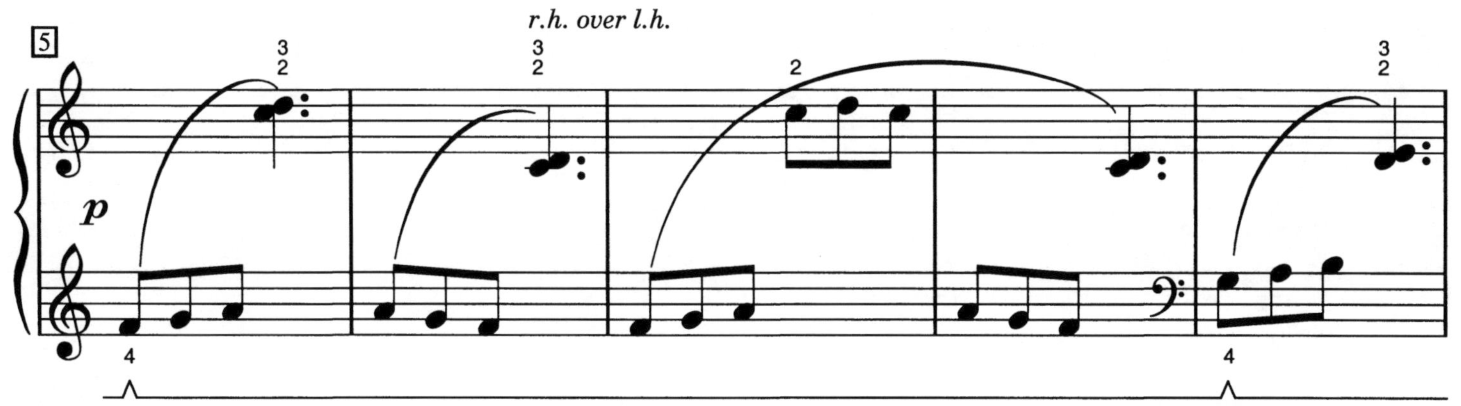

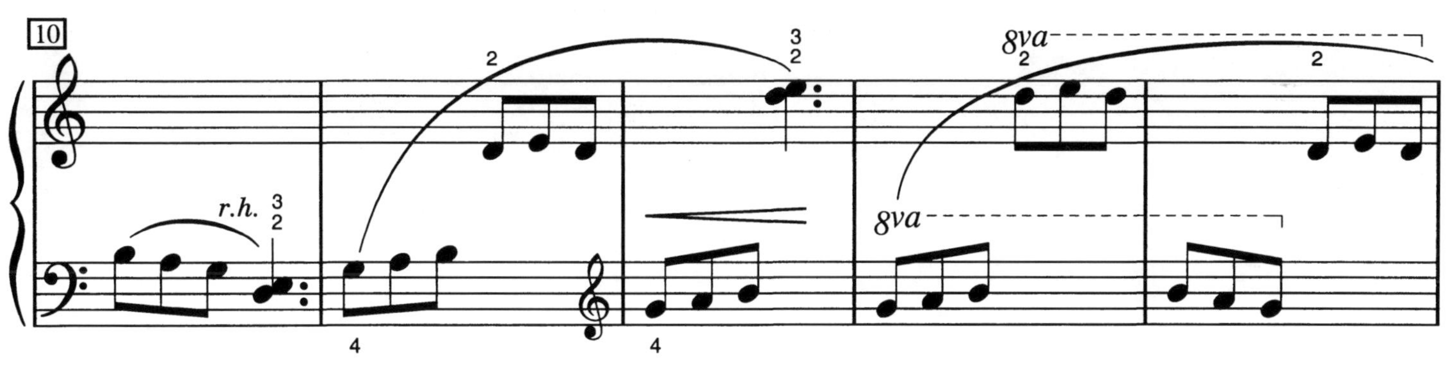

Arabian Knights

ELVINA PEARCE

Not fast, expressively

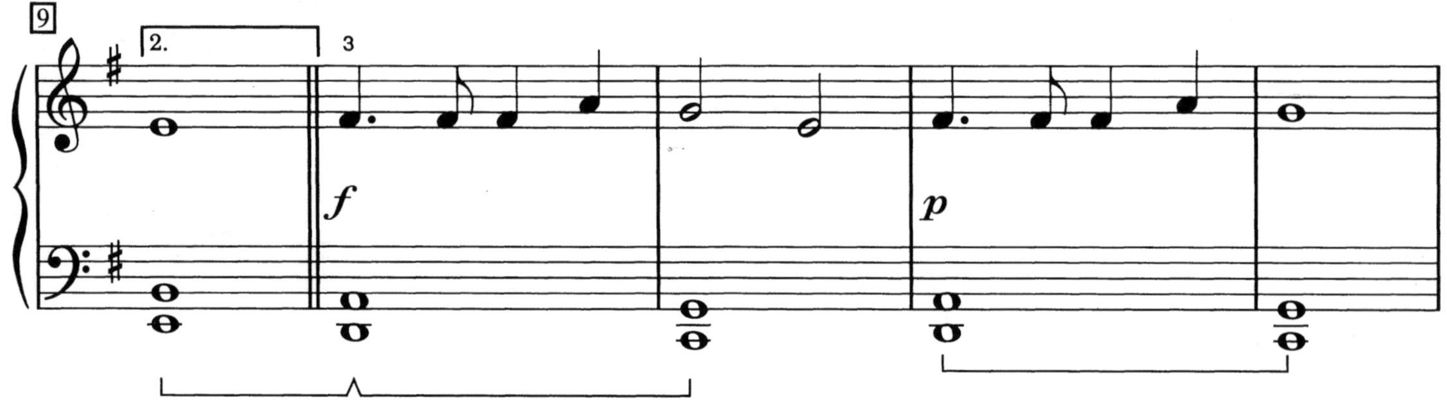

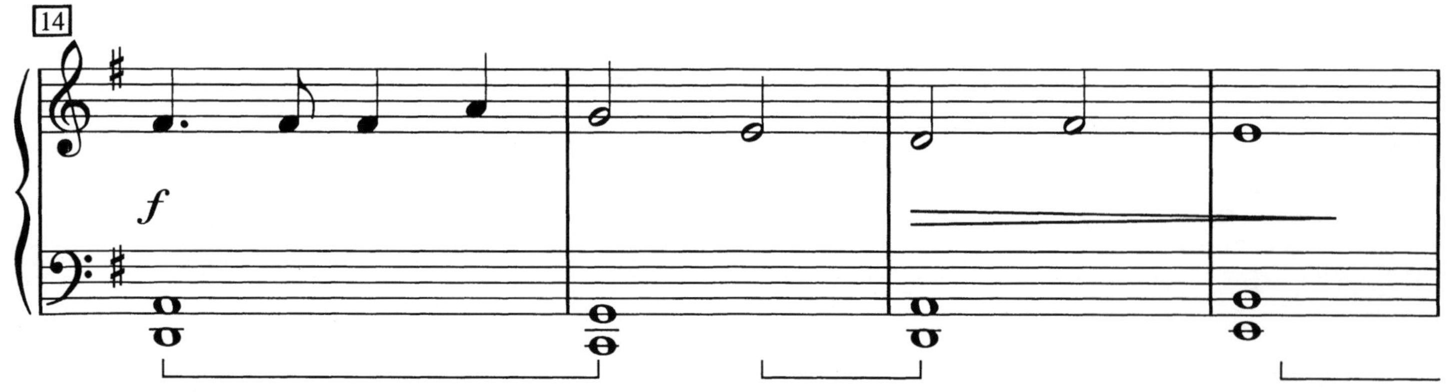

18
mp

22

26
mf

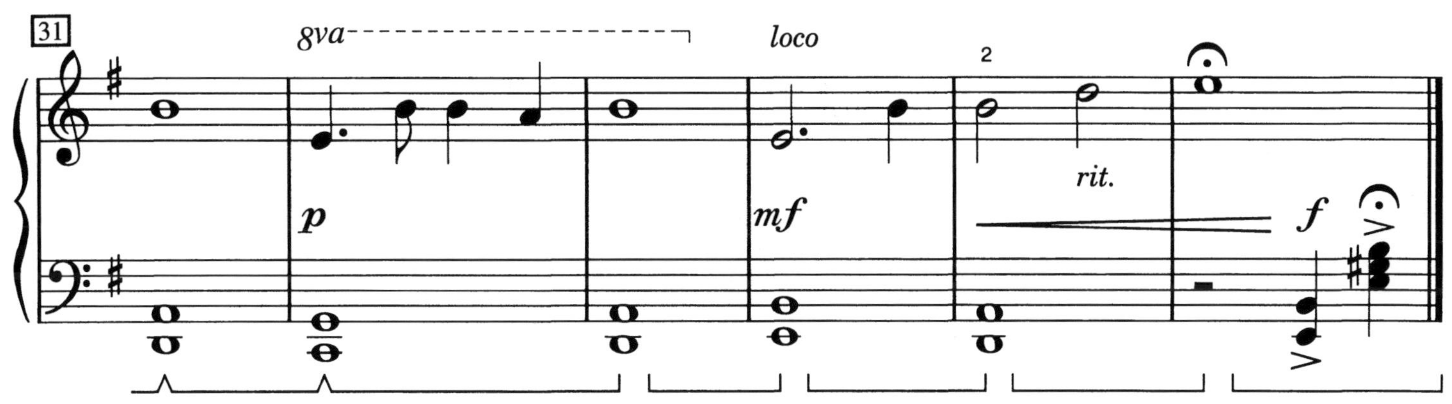
31
8va
loco
2
p
mf
rit.
f

Moon Dust

ELVINA PEARCE

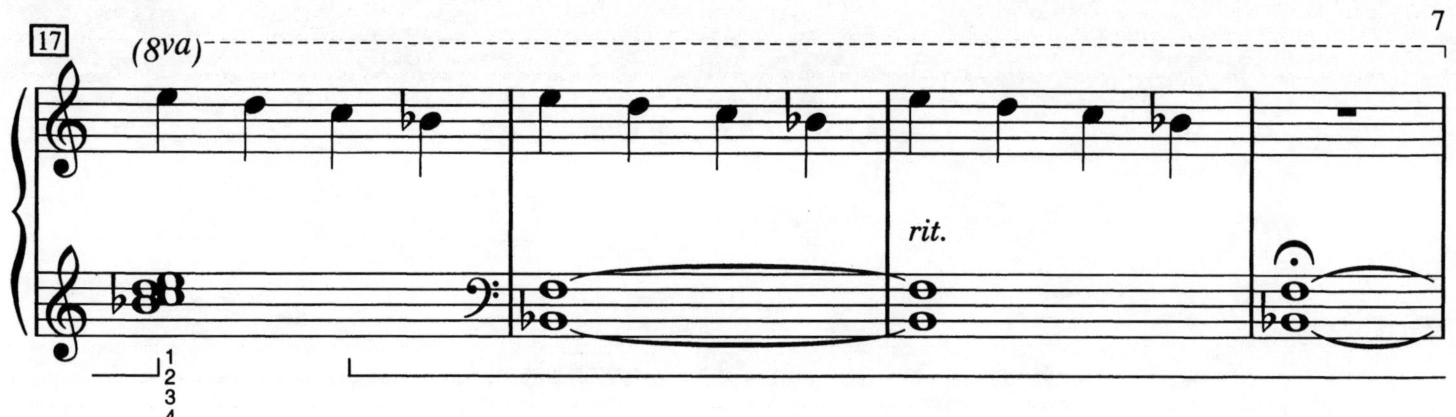

17
(8va)

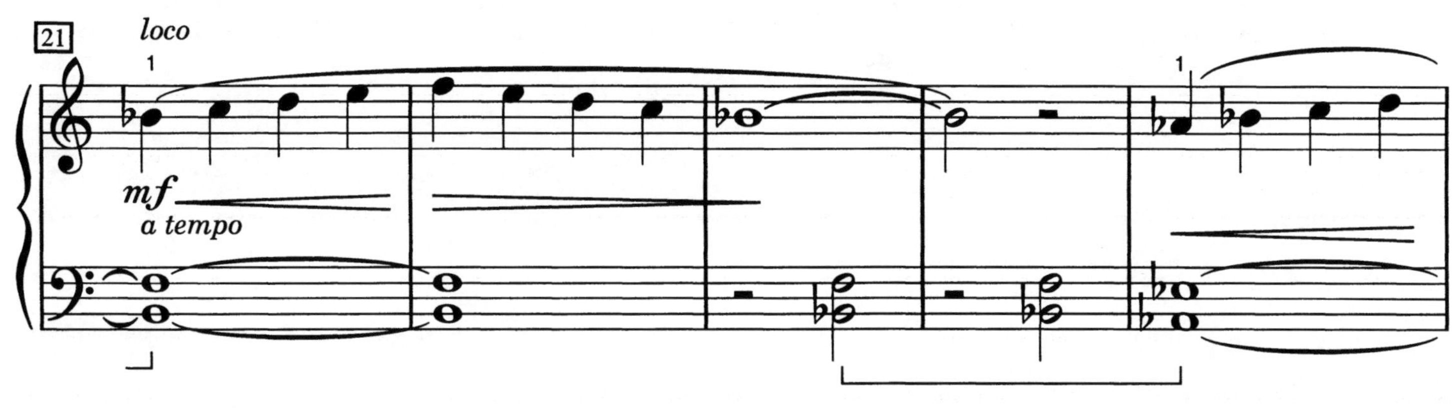

21
loco
mf
a tempo
rit.

26

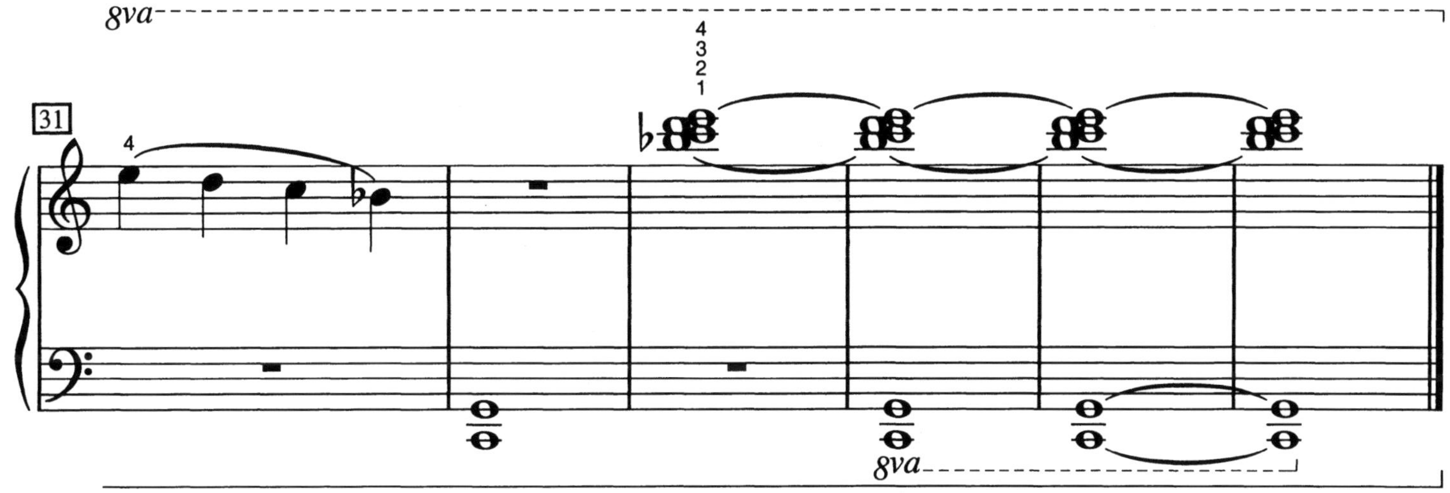

8va
31
8va

Joyful News

ELVINA PEARCE

13
pp
rit.

17
ff
a tempo

21

8va
25
mf
dim.

All Alone

ELVINA PEARCE

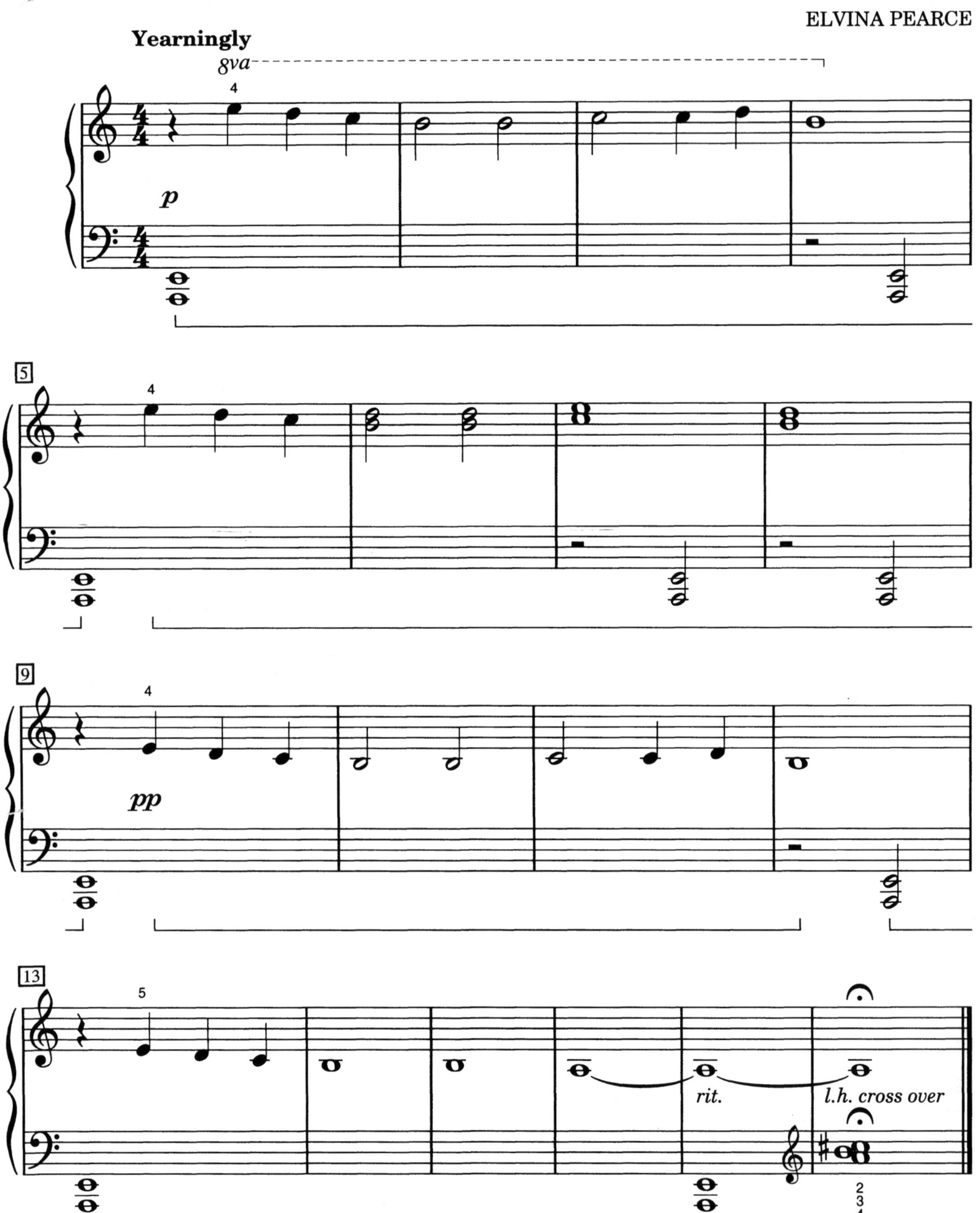

Autumn Haze

ELVINA PEARCE

Peaceful Journey

ELVINA PEARCE

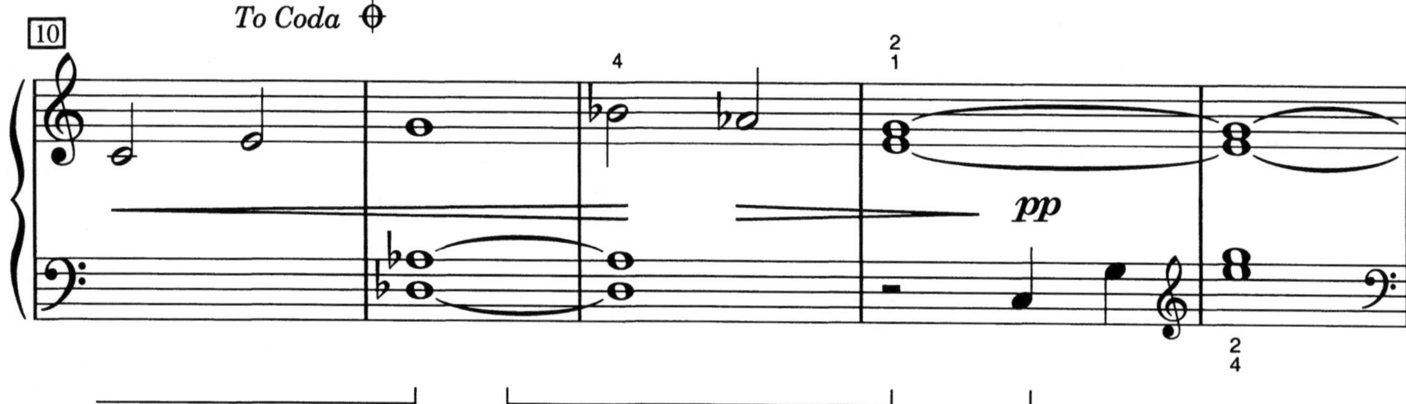

EL03706A

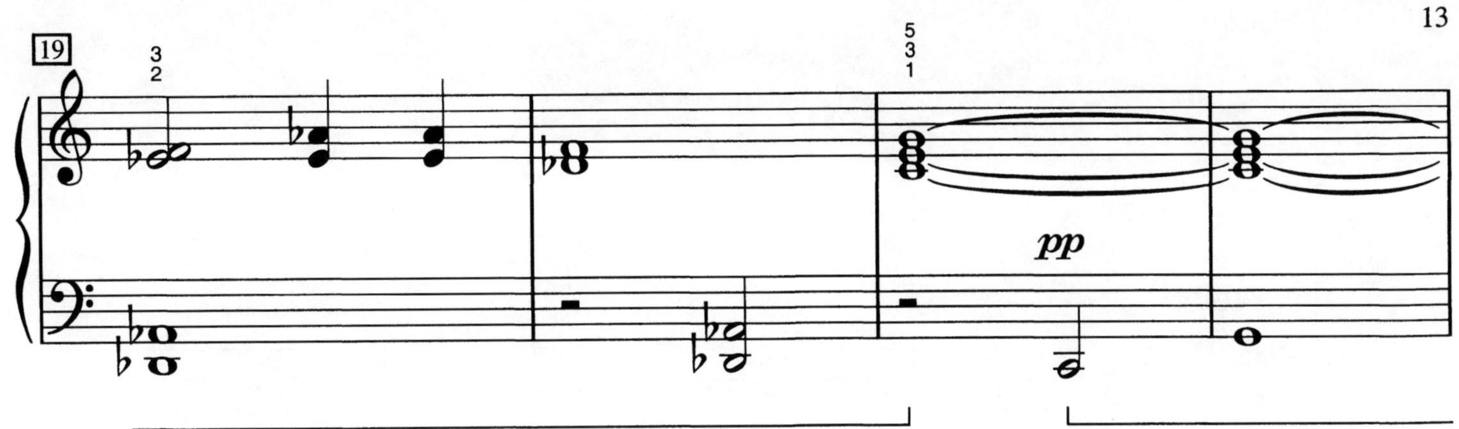
19
3
2
5
3
1
pp

23
4
p
2
1

D.C. al Coda
28
3
1
rit.
5

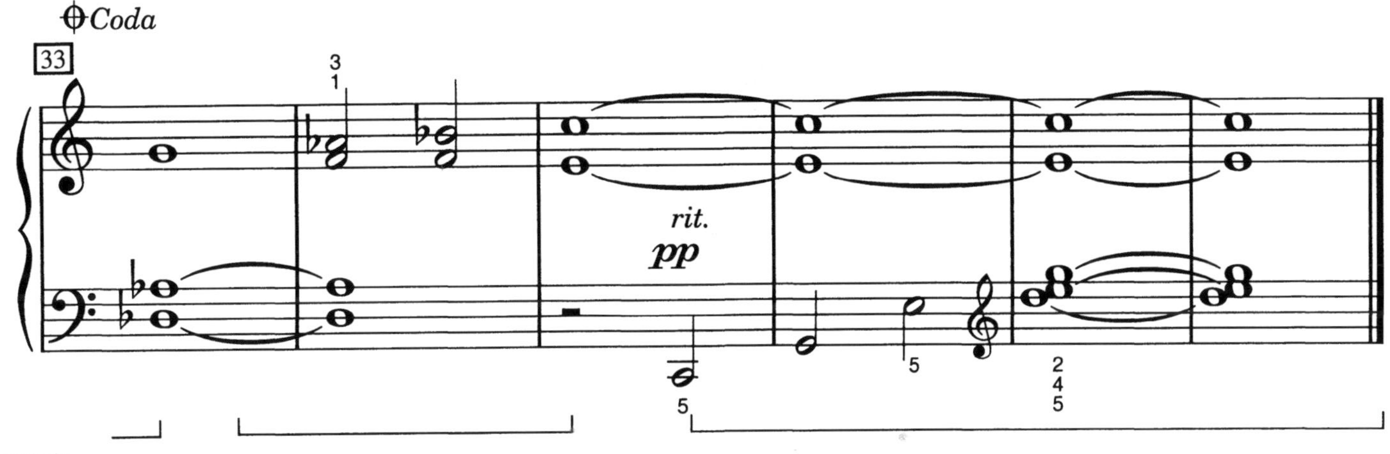
Coda
33
3
1
rit.
pp
5
5
2
4
5

Giant Steps

ELVINA PEARCE

15
ff

18

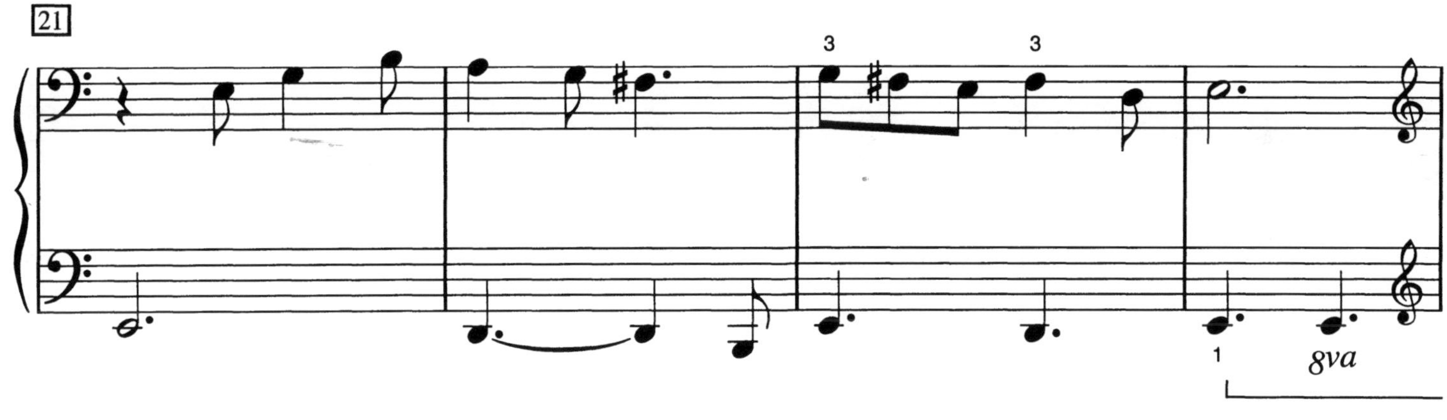
21
8va

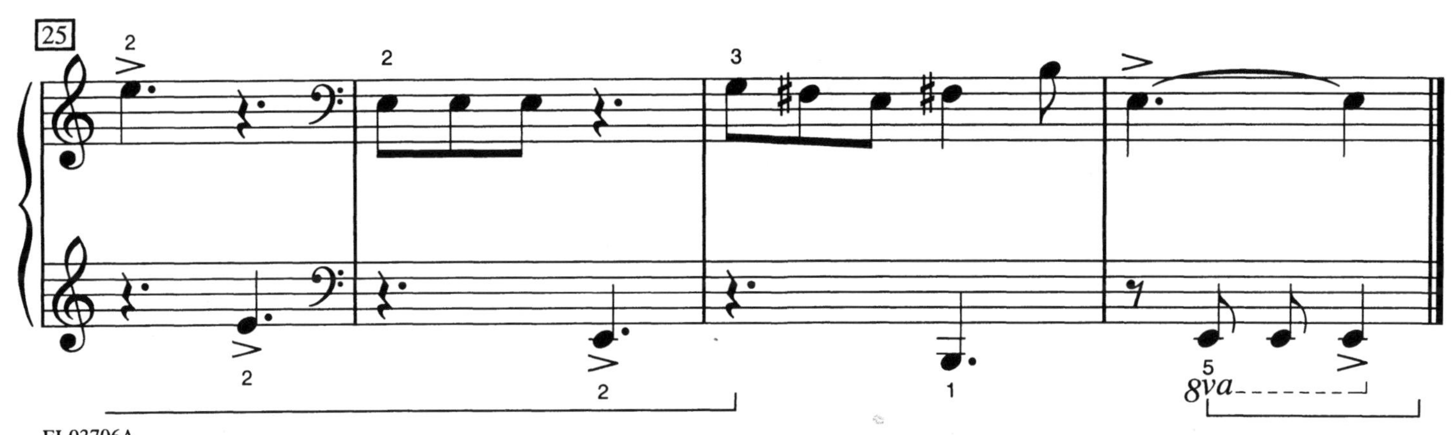
25
8va

Shifting Sands

ELVINA PEARCE

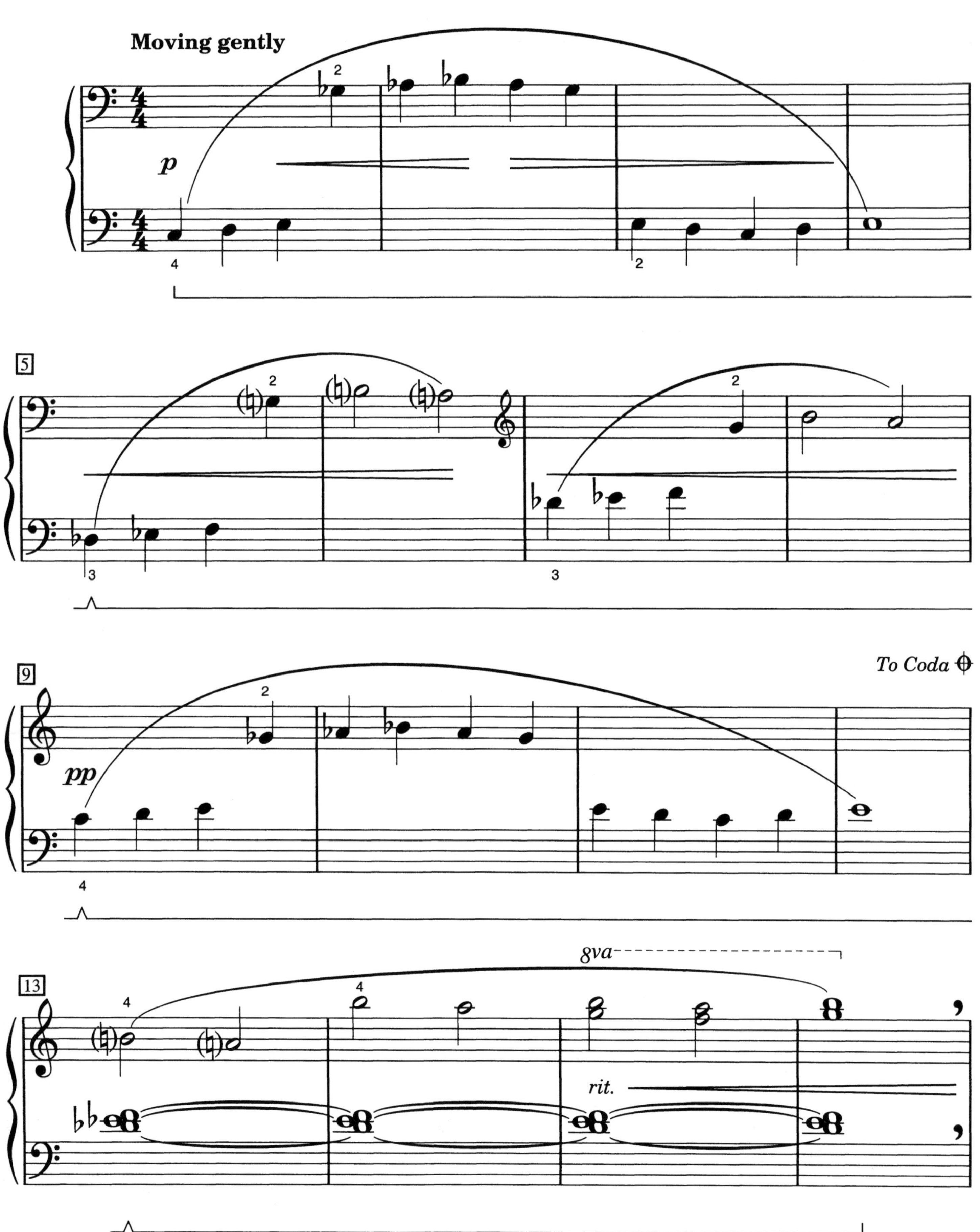

EL03706A

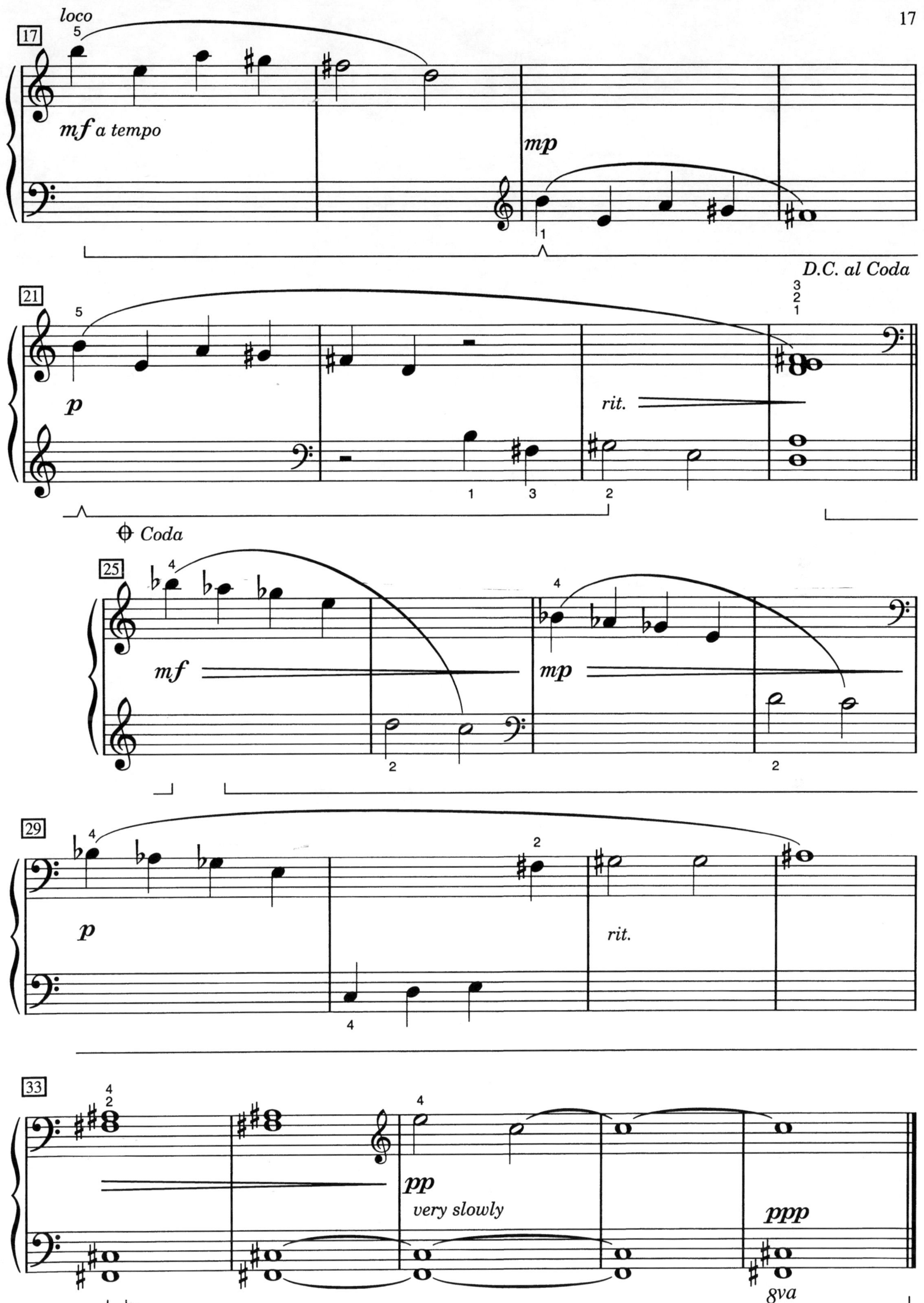
loco
mf a tempo
mp
D.C. al Coda
p
rit.
Coda
mf
mp
p
rit.
pp
very slowly
ppp
8va

Clown Shuffle

ELVINA PEARCE

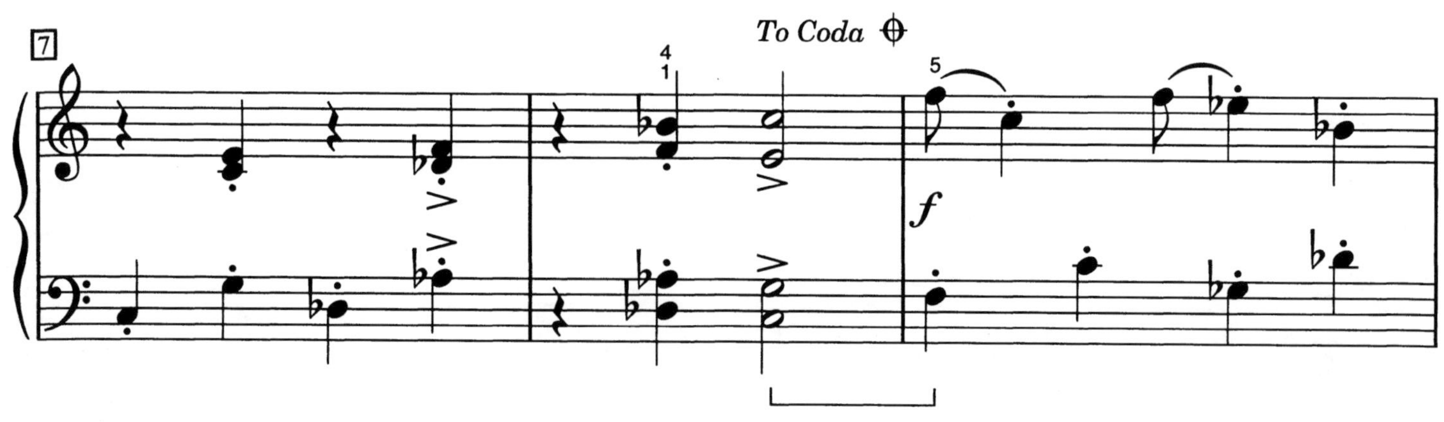

10

13
gva
f

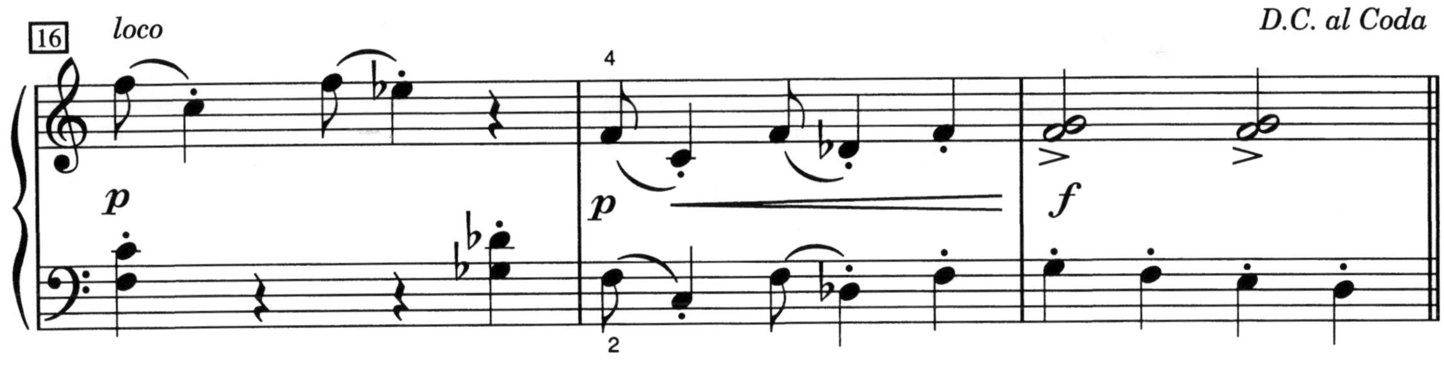
loco
D.C. al Coda
16
p
p
f

Coda
19
p
mp
mf
ff

Jogging

ELVINA PEARCE

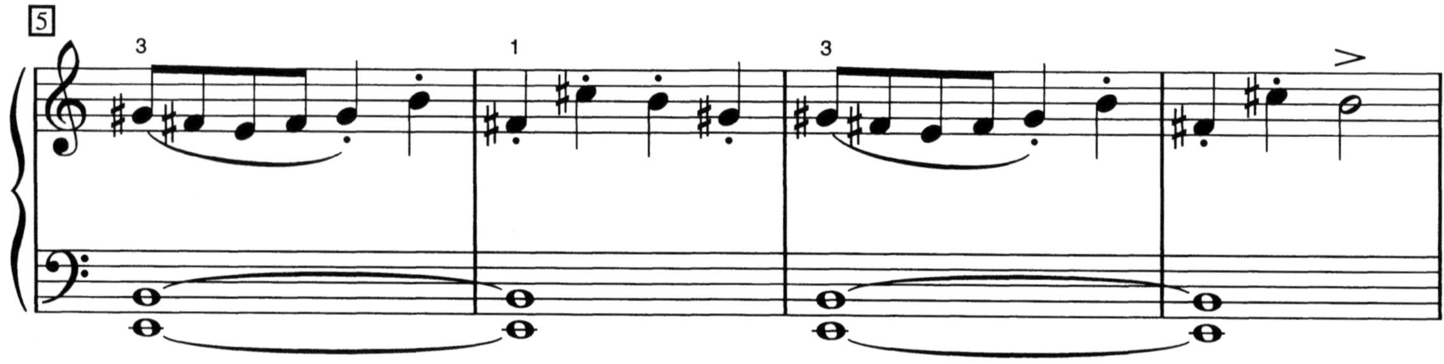

ELVINA TRUMAN PEARCE

Elvina Truman Pearce, pianist, teacher, lecturer, author, and composer, hails from Tulsa, Oklahoma, where she was a piano performance major at the University of Tulsa. She subsequently studied in New York City with the renowned Russian teacher Isabelle Vengerova, whose students included Samuel Barber, Leonard Bernstein, Lukas Foss, Gary Graffman, and Leonard Pennario.

Mrs. Pearce's solo concert career includes recitals at the National Gallery of Art in Washington, D.C., and at Carnegie Recital Hall in New York City. In addition, she has performed frequently as soloist with orchestras including the Amarillo Symphony, the Tulsa Philharmonic, and the Chicago Symphony, as well as the WGN Chicago Philharmonic in a coast-to-coast broadcast on the "Chicago Theater of the Air."

Following study in New York, Mrs. Pearce was appointed to the piano faculty of Westminster Choir College in Princeton, New Jersey. While residing in Princeton, she studied with Frances Clark, nationally acclaimed author and teacher of teachers. She subsequently became one of the founding faculty members of the New School for Music Study in Princeton, New Jersey, where she served as supervisor of piano pedagogy and private instruction.

A frequent contributor to national music journals, her articles on pedagogy have been featured in *The American Music Teacher, Clavier, Keyboard Arts*, the *Piano Teacher,* and the *Piano Quarterly*. She is also the composer of many published collections of piano solos.

For fourteen years Elvina Pearce taught piano pedagogy and directed the Preparatory Piano Division at Northwestern University. She currently lives in the western Chicago suburb of Naperville where she teaches at North Central College and serves as program consultant for the Division of Preparatory and Community Music, a program she founded and directed for eight years. In addition to teaching, writing, lecturing, and composing, Mrs. Pearce continues to perform as soloist with area orchestras, and she frequently presents lecture-recitals in conjunction with her workshops for teachers.